DATE DUE		
JUN 27 '84	2 1	APR 4 199
SEP 3 '85	OCT 19 '9	AY 7 — 19
MAR 7 '87	AUG 27 '9	
MAY 20 '87	SEP 2 '9	
SEP 21 '8	SEP 24 '92	
FEB -3 1990	UG 30 '93	
MAR 10 '90	OCT 5 9	
JUN 4 '90	R 1 1 '9	
FEB 18 '9	EP 07 199	
MAY 8 '9	OCT 24 199	
JUL 24 198	NOV 1 1994	
UG 7 20	DEC 14 1994	

THE SQUIRRELS

BY
JANA McCONOUGHEY

EDITED BY
DR. HOWARD SCHROEDER

**Professor in Reading and Language Arts
Dept. of Elementary Education
Mankato State University**

PRODUCED AND DESIGNED BY
BAKER STREET PRODUCTIONS
Mankato, MN

CRESTWOOD HOUSE
Mankato, Minnesota

LIBRARY OF CONGRESS CATALOGING IN PUBLICATION DATA
McConoughey, Jana
  The squirrels

  (Wildlife, habits and habitat)
  SUMMARY: Discusses the physical characteristics, habits, behavior, and distribution of the tree squirrel and also briefly discusses flying and ground squirrels.
  1. Squirrels--Juvenile literature. (1. Squirrels) I. Schroeder, Howard. II. Title.
QL737.R68M333   599.32'32   83-2085
ISBN 0-89686-223-2 (lib. bdg.)

International Standard Book Number:	Library of Congress Catalog Card Number:
Library Binding 0-89686-223-2	83-2085

ILLUSTRATION CREDITS:
Cheryl Todd: Cover
Fish and Wildlife Service: 5
National Park Service: 7
Lynn Rogers: 8, 9, 11, 21, 22, 28, 31, 34, 42-43
Phil and Loretta Hermann: 10, 12, 39
C. Summers/Tom Stack and Associates: 13
Rick Kolodziej: 15
Bob Williams: 16, 19, 24
Henry Kartarik: 27
Steve Kuchera: 33
Rod Planck/Tom Stack and Associates: 37

CRESTWOOD HOUSE
Hwy. 66 South, Box 3427
Mankato, MN 56002-3427

TABLE OF CONTENTS

INTRODUCTION:

Many years ago thick, green forests covered much of North America. These forests made a perfect home for rabbits, raccoons, wild turkeys, and many other animals. They were also home for millions of active little squirrels.

When the first settlers came to America, they quickly became acquainted with the squirrels. Once these pioneers had built their cabins on the new land, they began to clear fields and plant crops. But as their crops began to grow, squirrels swarmed from the forest and ate the grain. Squirrels soon became quite a problem for the settlers. Some places even paid a bounty for squirrels.

As more settlers came to America, large sections of forest were cut down and the fallen trees burned. More crops were planted. As the squirrels' home got smaller, so did the number of squirrels. They no longer swarmed into the fields to eat the grain. They were no longer a problem for the settlers.

The number of squirrels in America was greatly reduced by the settlers. However, many still lived in the forests that remained. Today, squirrels can be found almost everywhere in North America. In the country, or even the busy city, you can find squirrels. They live just about anywhere.

There are two main types of squirrels in North America. One type is the tree squirrels. These squirrels, as their name suggests, live in trees. They are easily recognized by their large, bushy tails which they use for balance as they leap from tree to tree. High in the trees they build their nests, raise their young, and sleep at night. When they are not doing these things, you can find them down on the ground, looking for seeds, nuts, and bugs to eat.

There are also ground squirrels in North America. These animals live in little burrows dug into the earth. They are very small with short, thin tails and dark stripes down their sides. A good place to find ground squirrels is in the ditches along country roads. They like to dig their burrows there. Because of their short thin tails, most people do not think of them as squirrels. Ground squirrels are discussed in Chapter Five of this book.

A tree squirrel shows its bushy tail.

CHAPTER ONE:

Tree squirrels

Tree squirrels are found over a large portion of North America. If there are trees in the area, there probably are tree squirrels, too. However, squirrels avoid the bitter cold of northern Canada, and the hot, humid region of southern Mexico.

Tree squirrels actively climb about the trees and forage for food during the day. They are busiest in the early morning and late afternoon. Squirrels are often on the ground at these times looking for something to eat. They spend the nights curled up in their nests, asleep. Because they sleep at night and are active during the day, tree squirrels are called diurnal animals.(One kind of tree squirrel, the flying squirrel, is an exception. It sleeps during the day.)

Tree squirrels are not aggressive animals, but are not very shy either. Squirrels living in areas where there are a lot of people can become quite tame. Those that live in parks and on college campuses may even eat from a person's hand. Squirrels do not usually fight with other animals or among themselves. A squirrel may become angry, though, if

This ground squirrel looks for a free lunch in a park in Alaska.

Although squirrels seldom fight, these red squirrels obviously disagree about something!

another animal or a human invades its territory. It will not attack the intruder. Instead, it will climb the nearest tree for safety. Then it will scold the invader with a loud, persistent chatter.

Types of North American tree squirrels

Some squirrels can glide through the air from one tree to another. These squirrels are called "flying squirrels." They are discussed in Chapter Five. Their habits are different from those of the non-flying tree squirrels. Non-flying tree squirrels all have similar habits. However, they look very different from each other.

The eastern gray squirrel can be found throughout the entire eastern half of the United States, and in extreme southern Canada. It is eight to thirteen inches (20-33 cm) long, with an additional seven to ten inches (13-25 cm) of bushy tail. Occasionally, its fur is black, but usually it is a shade of gray. White-tipped hairs often form a border around its tail.

An eastern gray squirrel.

The western gray squirrel is larger. It is twenty-two to twenty-four inches (56-61 cm) long, ten to twelve inches (25-33 cm) of which is tail. This squirrel is also gray, with a white belly that distinguishes it from the eastern gray. It lives only in parts of Washington, Oregon, California, and northern Mexico.

The fox squirrel looks very much like the gray squirrels. Its belly is usually more yellowish though, and it often has some black or white on its head. They can be nineteen to thirty inches long (48-76 cm), including a nine to fourteen inch (23-36 cm) tail. They may weigh up to three pounds (7 kg), twice as

A western gray squirrel.

A fox squirrel.

much as a gray squirrel. The fox squirrel dwells in the eastern United States and a small portion of southern Canada. Its range does not extend north of the Great Lakes region.

The squirrel which is most common is the red squirrel. It is found throughout Canada, except for the extreme northern areas. Its range also includes the northern half of the United States. Yellowish-reddish fur and a white belly distinguish this squirrel from other kinds. In the winter it is slightly more

11

A red squirrel.

gray, and in the summer it develops dark markings along its sides. It can be eleven to fourteen inches long (28-36 cm), including its four to six inch (10-15 cm) tail.

The most attractive squirrel in North America is the tassel-eared squirrel. This squirrel has tufts of long, thick fur at the tips of its ears. They are eighteen to twenty-two inches long (46-56 cm), eight or nine inches (20-23 cm) of which is tail. There are not many tassel-eared squirrels. They do not live in Canada. The only places in the United States where you

A tassel-eared squirrel.

can find them are Arizona, Colorado, New Mexico and southeastern Utah. They can also be found in northern and central Mexico. Tassel-eared squirrels are more varied in color than other squirrels. They have gray sides and brownish-gray backs. Their bellies can be either black or white. Those that live north of the Grand Canyon have tails that are all white. South of the Grand Canyon their tails are gray or brown with white underneath and along the sides.

Tails are important

The most outstanding feature of the tree squirrels is their tail. They have long, bushy tails that are often as long as their bodies. The fur on the tail is very thick and slightly longer than the body fur. The tail is quite flexible and can be bent into many positions. This makes the tail very useful to the tree squirrel.

Scientists call tree squirrels *Sciurus,* which means shade tail. This name is very appropriate. On hot summer days tree squirrels actually use their tails for shade. As they sit to eat a seed or nut, they hold their tail up over their back and head to block the sun.

Squirrels have other uses for their tails, too. In the rain the tail serves as an umbrella. In cold weather squirrels wrap it around them like a blanket. And, if a squirrel should happen to fall from a tree, its large tail catches the wind as it falls. This slows the animal's fall to the ground.

The most important use of the tail, though, is for balance. Squirrels spend much of their time sitting in the branches of trees. They sit on their hind feet, with their body bent forward and their tail behind them. The weight of their body is in front of their hind feet, and the weight of their large tail is behind them. In this way their weight is balanced evenly over their feet. They are able to sit quite steadily on thin and unsteady tree branches. Their tails can also help the squirrels when they leap onto nearby branches. The squirrels can shift their tails forward or backward when they land on the branch. This shifts their weight and can keep them from falling forward or backward off the branch.

A gray squirrel shades itself with its large tail.

Climbing abilities

It is not just their tails that make tree squirrels so well adapted to living in trees. These animals also have excellent jumping and climbing abilities. They have powerful hind legs that are longer and more muscular than their front legs. These strong legs allow them to jump from tree to tree. They also use them to climb up and down tree trunks and to jump about on the ground. All four feet have well developed "toes." With these toes, and the strong, sharp claws on each of them, tree squirrels can cling securely to the side of a tree.

The toes on a squirrels foot are made to hold onto trees and branches. The smaller inset shows the bottom of a front foot, and the other inset shows a back foot.

CHAPTER TWO:

The tree squirrel is a very active animal and is packed full of energy. It will eat about one hundred pounds of food a year. The average squirrel needs about two pounds of food a week. Most of its life is spent gathering food. Its diet consists of nuts, fruits, buds, seeds, berries, twigs and flowers. It is especially fond of corn. In general, its diet is very seasonal and depends on foods that are available.

Spring & summer — bits and pieces

In the spring and summer months the squirrel lives mostly on young tree buds and twigs. It will eat flower blossoms, berries and insects. Occasionally the squirrel also eats a bird's egg or some mushrooms. They eat all kinds of mushrooms, even those that are poisonous to humans. The squirrel's body is able to neutralize the poison in these mushrooms.

Fall — a lot to choose from

Fall is a good time of year for the tree squirrel because it can dine on nuts and corn. Trees bearing walnuts, hickory nuts, hazelnuts and acorns are found throughout much of the United States, Canada and central Mexico. These nuts are a favorite food of the tree squirrel. It spends much of its day on the ground looking for them. When it finds one it sniffs it. By smelling a nut, the squirrel can tell if there are worms in it. If there are, it tosses the nut away. If it is a good nut, the squirrel usually takes it in its mouth and climbs up into a tree to eat it. As it holds the nut in its paws, it gnaws a hole into it with its bottom teeth. These two teeth are long and thin, and very strong. When the squirrel has made a hole in the nut, it pushes these teeth into the hole and pries the nut open. Once the squirrel has the nut open, it again uses its long bottom teeth. It picks the nut out of the shell with them. Then it lets the empty shell fall to the ground. The squirrel's teeth are obviously very important for survival. Gnawing on nuts keeps them clean and sharp.

In areas where pine trees grow, a tree squirrel will feed on pine cones. First, the squirrel grabs at a pine cone that is within its reach using its paws. It then separates the cone from the tree with a quick bite and carries it to a sturdy branch where it can sit comfortably and eat it. The squirrel begins eating a cone by ripping the scales off the cone with its teeth. Beneath each scale is a seed which the squirrel licks out with its tongue and then eats. It works very quickly. Animal ecologists have seen squirrels strip as many as 190 cones in one day.

Besides being a plentiful season for the tree squirrel, fall is also a busy one. It is the season when the squirrel must gather up extra food and store it away for the winter. It spends fall days hiding nuts, pine cones, and seeds that it finds.

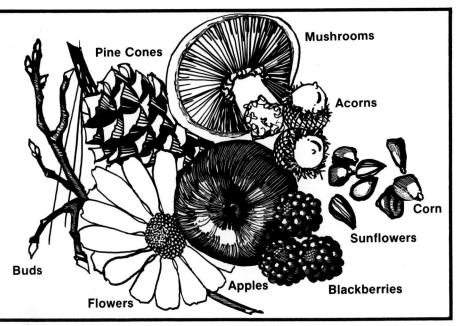

Some typical tree squirrel foods.

When the squirrel finds a nut or another bit of food that it wants to hide, it digs a small hole in the ground with its front feet. If it is hiding a nut or cone that it has chewed off a tree, it digs a hole at the base of that tree and buries it. The tree squirrel is not very picky about where it hides its "treasures." It usually hides them close to where it finds them. Once it has dug a hole, the squirrel places the food it has found inside. Then it packs it down tightly into the ground with its teeth. Finally, the squirrel gathers soil and leaves with its forelegs and places them in the hole. It packs the dirt and leaves with its feet, then scurries off to find another nut or seed to eat or bury. One squirrel will bury as many as forty nuts in an hour. When winter comes it will not remember where it buried all of the nuts. Instead, it will use its keen sense of smell to find them.

Winter — time to dig

Food is scarce for a tree squirrel in the winter. There are no fruits, berries or insects to eat. It does eat some twigs and tree bark in the winter. However, it relies almost totally on the nuts and cones that were buried in the fall. It sniffs the ground for the buried food. A squirrel eats any food it can find,

A gray squirrel eats food that was buried in the fall.

whether or not it was the one who buried it. In this way squirrels share their food. It is not always the same squirrel who buried the nut that gets to eat it.

Most of the nuts and cones that were buried in the fall are dug up and eaten by hungry squirrels. Squirrels are very good at finding them. Their sense of smell is well developed. They can smell a pine cone twelve inches (30 cm) beneath the snow. However, each year there are a few nuts and seeds that go undetected. These sprout in the spring and grow into new trees. Many tall, beautiful trees have been planted in this way.

CHAPTER THREE:

Nest building

The tree squirrel usually lives alone, at the top of an old and steady tree. It prefers to build its nest inside a hollow part of the tree. A squirrel will often use an abandoned woodpecker's hole as its new home. Squirrels do not gnaw their own holes in trees.

The hole in this tree leads to a gray squirrel's nest.

If one cannot find an abandoned hollow tree, it will build a nest of leaves in the branches. If it does find a hollow tree for its home, the squirrel first lines the hollow with dried leaves. Then it adds finely shredded tree bark. It packs the bark into a soft, round bowl. Most of these nests are just large enough for one squirrel. However, some females make their nests slightly larger so that they can raise their babies in them.

The tree squirrel is also skilled at making leaf nests. It builds these nests in the fork of two strong tree branches. The floor of the nests is much like that of a bird's nest. In fact, many times a squirrel will use an old bird nest for its floor. If there are no bird nests available though, it makes its own by plastering twigs and leaves together with mud. A squirrel may have to travel to a nearby stream or river to get the mud it needs. It scrapes mud from the ground with its front feet and carries it to its nest in its mouth. Then it uses leaves, moss, and the mud to build the walls and ceiling of its new home. The inside of the nest is lined with grass, husks, feathers, moss, and even paper. When finished, a squirrel's nest may measure up to twenty inches (50 cm) across the outside. It may be twelve inches (30 cm) high.

Leaf nests have one main entrance hole. Opposite the entrance, the squirrel makes another smaller hole which it uses as an "escape hatch." Raccoons and snakes are enemies of the North American tree

A drawing showing a cross section of a leaf nest. The main entrance is on the left and the escape hole is on the right.

squirrel. Many times raccoons reach into the squirrel's nest in search of a quick meal. Rat snakes, which live throughout the Midwest and eastern half of the United States, often crawl into the nest looking for food as well. When this happens, the squirrel can escape from its nest by using the escape hole. Owls and hawks are also enemies of the tree squirrels, but rarely enter the squirrel's nest. Instead, they attack the squirrel from the air.

Sometimes a squirrel will build several smaller nests besides its main nest. It builds these nests at varying distances away from the main nest. If the food supply near the main nests runs short, it can travel to its smaller nests and look for food there.

Another reason for building the other nests is for protection. When the squirrel is away from its main nest it can escape a hungry hawk or owl by hiding in one of these other nests.

Getting together

Squirrels usually live alone in their nests. However, they do enjoy each other's company during the daytime hours. Many times they can be seen playfully chasing each other through the trees. After a squirrel has chased another squirrel for some time, it may turn around and let the other squirrel chase it. When the squirrels have worked off their extra energy, they will simply stop the chase and resume searching for food. Often a squirrel will start to chatter from its perch up in the tree. The other squirrels in the trees around it will join in. They all sit and chatter loudly at each other, for no other reason than to inform the others of their presence.

There are times when squirrels do share their nests with one another. To keep warm in the winter, they will squeeze tightly together in a single nest. They will wrap their tails around each other for extra warmth. In severe winter weather they will huddle together for days, and not go outside. Squirrels will also share their nest with their mate for a short time during the mating season.

Room to live

If there is enough food, a squirrel will stay close to its nest throughout the year. It will not usually travel more than a quarter of a mile away from its home nest. Biologists have caught squirrels and put tags on their ears. Then they moved the squirrels as far as three miles away from their homes. They wanted to see if the animals would find their homes again. Within a few days all of the squirrels were back in their nests.

Although squirrels would rather stay near their homes, they are not always able to. Sometimes the area where they live acquires so many squirrels that there is not enough food to go around. Then they must move to a new area. Many squirrels may leave an area at the same time to look for new homes.

Occasionally there are food shortages for squirrels over large areas of North America. In 1968, there was a mass migration in the eastern part of the

Melanistic (black) gray squirrels are unusual, but not really rare.

United States. Campers and motorists reported seeing hundreds of squirrels hurrying through the woods and across roads toward the west. Boaters also saw large numbers of squirrels swimming across lakes and ponds. Biologists watched the mass migration of squirrels and estimated that eighty million squirrels left their homes and traveled as far as a hundred miles to find a new home. Migrations of this many squirrels are, of course, rare. Usually a squirrel only needs to go an extra mile or so away from its home to find enough food.

Albino (white) squirrels are quite rare.

CHAPTER FOUR:

Courtship and mating

Most tree squirrels have one mating season per year that lasts from spring through summer. However, some gray squirrels may mate once during the spring and again in midwinter.

Normally, the males stay in their own territories. During the mating season the males become aggressive and continually invade the female's territory. When a male enters a female's territory, the female becomes quite angry. She chatters at him loudly, but keeps her distance. The male does not heed the female's threats. Instead of leaving, he runs after her.

At first the female runs and tries to get away from the male. But after a short distance, she gives up trying to escape and is no longer angry at him. The chase then turns into play. Eventually the male runs ahead of the female. He stands so that she is sideways to him. This shows that he is ready to mate. He waves his tail back and forth several times. Then he slowly lays it on his back. If the female is ready to mate she lifts her tail straight into the air.

If the female is not ready to mate, the two squirrels

will chase each other and play together until she is. This playful courtship may last for several hours or for several days. The two squirrels stay close together during this time and share the same nest. Once the two have mated, the courtship ends. The female chases the male out of her nest and he returns to his own home. The two squirrels may never see each other again. The male will have no part in the raising of the young.

Caring for the young

The female's pregnancy lasts for thirty-eight days. She becomes very irritable and angrily chases away any squirrels that happen to wander near. When the thirty-eight days are over, she will give birth to anywhere from three to eight young. The average size litter for tree squirrels is five.

Baby squirrels are born pink and hairless. They are very tiny, weighing only about half an ounce at birth, and are only two inches (5 cm) long. Their heads and feet look too big for their tiny bodies. They are very helpless and rely on their mother's body heat to keep them warm. The mother keeps her babies very clean. She holds them in her forefeet and licks them. The mother squirrel stays in her nest with her young as much as she can. She leaves only to eat or drink.

Mother squirrels will attack enemies who come too near the nest. They have been known to leap onto people and scratch and bite them. They have also been known to attack snakes that are crawling toward their nest. Young squirrels are a favorite food of rat snakes. A mother squirrel was once seen jumping onto a rat snake and biting it on the head. Then she shook the snake loose from the tree and dropped it on the ground. The squirrel was still not satisfied and she ran to the ground and shook the snake some more! Then she rushed back up the tree to her young.

A mother squirrel keeps a sharp lookout when she has babies to protect.

Growing up

After squirrels are born they grow very slowly. Around ten to thirteen days they begin to grow fur. By nineteen days they are completely covered with fur. The young begin to hear after twenty-eight days, but do not open their eyes until they are thirty to thirty-two days old. At the same time they begin to grow teeth. After thirty-five days the young begin to clean themselves and gnaw on bits of bark in the nest. But their only source of food is the mother's milk until they are forty to forty-five days old. At that time they taste their first solid food by eating bits of what the mother brings into the nest to eat. It is around this time the young squirrels leave the nest for the first time.

The ages at which a baby squirrel develops may vary slightly among the different types of tree squirrels. Most baby squirrels, though, are weaned from their mother when they are about eight weeks old. This means they no longer nurse from their mother. Now they must find their own food.

After young squirrels are weaned they spend much time playing in trees. The mother also begins to encourage her babies to learn to climb. She leads them on journeys through the tree branches in single file. The babies are always anxious to follow their mother since they do not want to be left behind.

Two young squirrels come out of their nest in a birch tree.

33

They learn to jump from branch to branch as they follow her through the trees.

When the young squirrels have learned to be good tree climbers, the mother leads them down to the ground. There they look for food together. The baby squirrels do not have to be taught how to search for food or how to eat nuts and seeds. They know these things by instinct. This means that, by nature, they begin searching for seeds and nuts when they reach the ground.

Young squirrels may stay with their mothers for some time. They may even live with their mothers until she has her next litter. Usually, the mother chases the babies out of her nest when they are several months old. The young squirrels then leave to find new homes in other places. Wherever the squirrels choose to build their new homes, they will probably remain there for the full ten to twelve years of their lives.

This gray squirrel is gathering seeds from a box elder tree. It's all in a day's work!

CHAPTER FIVE:

Flying squirrels

Some tree squirrels are called flying squirrels. Flying squirrels live over the eastern half of the United States and over most of Canada. They also live in central Mexico. They do not really fly, as their name implies. But have large flaps of skin along their sides that allow them to glide through the air from tree to tree. Many people have never seen a flying squirrel. That's because they are nocturnal animals, which means they sleep during the day and are active at night. Zoos, however, usually have flying squirrels for people to see.

Flying squirrels look very much like other tree squirrels. Their bodies are smaller though, measuring only about six inches (15.4 cm) long. They have large dark eyes. These eyes are made for seeing in the dark. A flying squirrel has very good eyesight. It also has a bushy tail similar to other tree squirrels. However, it is not usually quite as long and the fur is parted in the middle. Because of this, their tail looks flat. They use this tail as a rudder when they glide through the air.

When a flying squirrel wishes to "fly," it launches

itself from the top of a tall tree. The squirrel extends its legs. The fur-covered skin flap, called a patagium, stretches from the wrists on its front legs to its ankles. The patagium is pulled tight and acts like a parachute. The squirrel can then glide through the air. Sometimes it can glide 150 feet (46.7 m) at a time! By moving its feet and tail, it can change direction in the air. This comes in handy when it is trying to escape a hungry owl, the flying squirrel's main enemy.

Flying squirrels build their nest inside hollow trees twenty to thirty feet above the ground. Usually they take over abandoned woodpecker nests. They line their nest inside with bark, leaves, and moss, much like other tree squirrels. They also live in their nests alone. However, as many as twelve of them will huddle in a single nest during cold, winter weather.

The diet of the flying squirrel is much like that of other tree squirrels. They eat nuts, seeds, blossoms, buds, berries, insects, grain, and mushrooms. They may also bury nuts in the ground. Usually, though, they keep their extra food in tree hollows.

Mating season for the flying squirrel is in the late winter. Babies are born in March or April. They are very tiny at birth. Five of them together weigh about an ounce. Baby flying squirrels are hairless and blind at birth just like other tree squirrels. But they grow much faster. By the time they are six weeks old they can leave the nest and begin to gather their own food.

This photo of a flying squirrel shows its patagium, the flap of skin between its front "wrist" and rear "ankle."

Female flying squirrels are devoted mothers. They nurse their babies every hour. When their babies are in danger they move them to a new nest. Instead of carrying them across tree branches and over the ground, she flies them to their new home. Nothing gets in a mother squirrel's way when she is protecting her babies and moving them about. There is a reported case of a woodsman who once chopped down a tree that had a nest of young flying squirrels in it. The man was curious to see what the mother squirrel would do. He picked up the baby squirrels and held them in his hands. The mother squirrel ran up his pant leg and took one of her babies in her mouth. Then she carried it off to another tree and placed it inside a vacant hole. She showed no fear of the man at all, and did not bite or scratch him. She simply retrieved her babies one by one without hesitation until they were all moved to a new home!

Ground squirrels

There are also ground squirrels in North America. These squirrels are very different from tree squirrels. Many people don't even think of them as squirrels. They do not have the large bushy tails that tree squirrels have. And they live in burrows which they dig into the ground. Ground squirrels eat much the same things that tree squirrels do. They are also very energetic like tree squirrels.

Ground squirrels are found almost everywhere in the United States. In fact, the only place where they don't live in North America is in the extreme northern parts of Canada, and the extreme southern parts

A golden-manteled ground squirrel.

of Mexico. They are often seen in most parks and woodland areas.

Ground squirrels are small animals with brown to reddish-brown fur. Some have white and black stripes down their sides. They live in burrows that they dig just below the ground's surface. These tunnels are quite elaborate and may be twenty to thirty feet long. A ground squirrel will have several nests inside its burrow. It lines them with leaves, moss, and feathers just as tree squirrels do. There are also several spots in the tunnel where the ground squirrel stores its extra food. Acorns are a favorite food of ground squirrels. They also like to eat insects, mushrooms, snails, and many types of nuts. They love blackberries and raspberries! Occasionally they will kill and eat a small snake. Large snakes, though, are the ground squirrel's main enemy.

Mating season is in late March for most ground squirrels. Thirty-two days after a male and female have mated, usually four babies are born. The mother raises them herself, with no help from the father. The babies are tiny and helpless just like other squirrel babies. They stay in their mother's burrow until they are three months old.

At three months of age the young ground squirrels become independent. They leave their mother and look for a new place to live. Each will build its own burrow, and most likely never share it with another squirrel. Even during the cold winter months, ground squirrels do not huddle together like tree squirrels do. Instead they curl up in their tunnels and go to sleep. They stay asleep all winter, waking up occasionally to eat some of the food they have stored in their tunnels. When spring comes, the little ground squirrels will climb out of their burrow. Then they resume their life of gathering nuts and eating berries.

CHAPTER SIX:

Backyard "pets"

You may happen to have squirrels living in your backyard. If so, you are very lucky. Squirrels can provide you with hours of entertainment. Try filling a bird feeder with corn or nuts. You will have fun watching the lively little animals scurry around. If you want to make a squirrel happy, put out some peanut butter. Squirrels really like peanut butter! Once it has accepted you and knows that you have food for it, it will stay close to your house.

If you have never seen a squirrel and would like to, the first place to look is in a wooded area. Go to the park if there are no woods around. Check the ground around the trunks of trees for bits of empty nut shells. A tree with empty nut shells around it probably has a squirrel living in it. You may not see the squirrel at first. Sit down several yards away and wait patiently. Eventually the squirrels in the area will accept you as a part of the scenery. They will come out of hiding and go about their business.

Hunting

There are so many squirrels in North America that hunting them does not reduce their number much. In fact, there are so many squirrels that hunters actually help the squirrels by hunting them. Often times there is not enough food for all the squirrels in an

This red squirrel is very curious about photographyer Lynn Rogers' camera.

area, and many of them starve. It is better that some are killed and eaten. Then those remaining get the food they need to survive.

Most states allow squirrel hunting during a certain season. This hunting season usually lasts from September to January. It is illegal to hunt squirrels at any other time.

TREE SQUIRRELS

Eastern Gray, Western Gray, Tassel-Eared

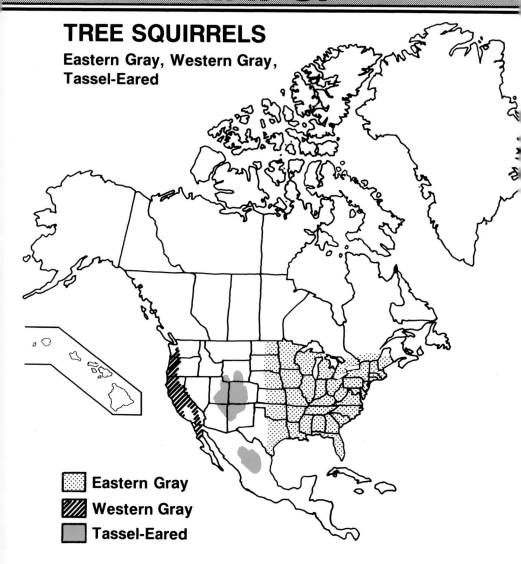

Eastern Gray

Western Gray

Tassel-Eared

TREE SQUIRRELS
Red, Fox, Flying

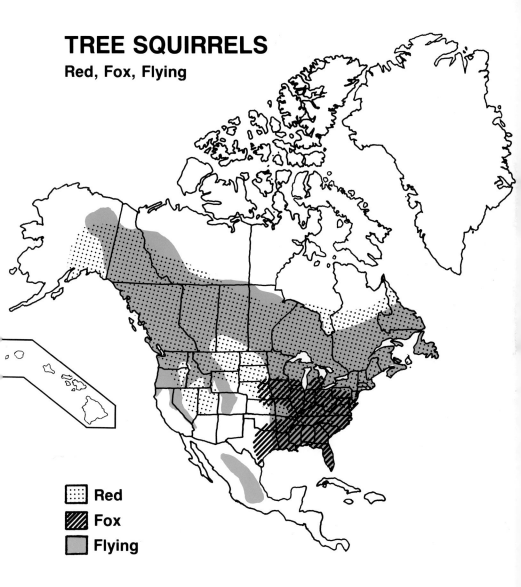

Red

Fox

Flying

GROUND SQUIRRELS

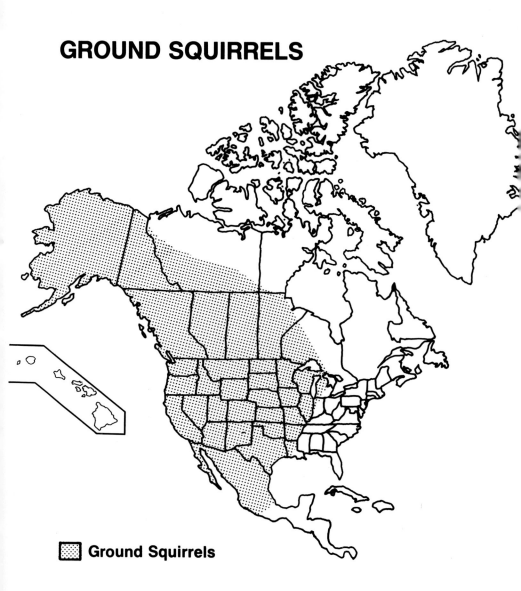

▨ **Ground Squirrels**

GLOSSARY:

ANIMAL ECOLOGISTS - A biologist who works specifically with animals.

BUD - A bump on the stem of a plant that may grow into a flower or leaf.

BURROW - A tunnel that an animal digs in the ground.

COURTSHIP - When an animal acts a certain way so that it can attract a mate.

DIURNAL ANIMAL - An animal that is active in the day and inactive, or asleep, in the night.

FORAGE - To look for food.

INSTINCT - An impulse or tendency for an animal to act a certain way.

MIGRATE - To travel from one region to another for feeding or breeding.

NEUTRALIZE - The ability to counteract the activity or effect of a chemical

NOCTURNAL ANIMAL - An animal that is active in the night and inactive or asleep, in the day.

PATAGIUM - A flap of skin that connects the front and back legs of a flying squirrel.

RUDDER - A flat appendage that is used to change an object's or animal's direction while it is flying or moving.